This book is
the las

D0533899

You've got your own bed.
So why die in someone else's?

**Find out how Marie Curie Nurses
can help you. www.mariecurie.org.uk**

Dying to know

Dedicated to Tim and Blue, Kerry Hancock, Susie Smith, Polly Campbell,
Kyah Woodhill, Ben Padfield, Matthew Anastasios and their families.

First published in the United Kingdom in 2010
by Hardie Grant Books London

Published in 2007
by Pilotlight Australia in conjunction with Hardie Grant Books
85 High Street
Prahran, Victoria
3181, Australia
www.hardiegrant.com.au

ISBN 9781740665537

Cover photographs courtesy Pat LaCroix/Getty Images (front)
and iStockphoto (back)

Printed and bound by C & C Offset Printing

10 9 8 7 6 5 4 3 2 1

Dying to know
Bringing death to life

Conceived and brought together by Pilotlight Australia, with a view to connecting us all a little bit more.

Creative Team Jane Tewson, Andrew Knight, Andrew Anastasios, Jo Lane, Stephanie Exton
Written by Andrew Anastasios
Designed by Trisha Garner and Michelle Mackintosh

As with all our initiatives, *Dying to Know* has been made possible by extensive pro bono support including from the members of the creative team and our friends at Hardie Grant, Sandy Grant, Julie Pinkham and Jane Aspden.

hardie grant books
MELBOURNE · LONDON

Like so many others, we have been challenged by death and what lies beyond it. People have always lived with death – immediate, visible, an inseparable part of life. Death and its rituals have been played out in private and in public, as part of the language and experience of all.

But for many of us today, death is feared and has become, somewhat ironically in this permissive age, a modern taboo. We push away all signs of encroaching mortality and increasingly relegate older people to the fringes of our society, their collective wisdom wasted.

At Pilotlight Australia we believe that renewing a conversation about dying can help build supportive communities and inspire change for the living.
Dying to Know seeks to break the silence around death and dying and stimulate a discussion that genuinely connects people on the most profound level, not as experts, but as people with the same dreams, hopes, fears and concerns.

Pilotlight Australia is a not-for-profit organisation committed to igniting social change.

Dying to Know offers 60 thoughts that reflect on **bringing death to life**. It would not have been possible without significant and heartfelt input from a wide range of individuals and organisations with whom we have been privileged to share our ideas. These include children, palliative care workers, people with terminal illness, funeral industry professionals, religious leaders, philosophers, doctors, those who have lost loved ones, and many friends.

We hope ***Dying to Know*** offers ideas for everyone to make a difference to themselves and the lives of others.

Jane Tewson CBE

The meaning of life?

People study for weeks for a birth.
Why not study for a death?

We have no shortage of names for it:

passing away ∗ snuffing it ∗ starting a worm farm
∗ staring at the lid ∗ meeting your maker ∗ kicking
the bucket ∗ croaking ∗ giving up the ghost ∗
dropping off ∗ pushing up daisies ∗ cashing in
your chips ∗ turning up your toes ∗ going to the
happy hunting ground ∗ going to God ∗ putting
down your knife and fork ∗ bowing out ∗ shuffling
off ∗ taking your last breath ∗

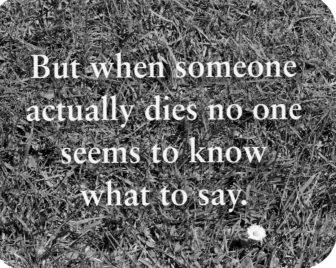

If
you knew
when it was
coming,
would you do
anything
differently?

Why wait?

Don't try to be too profound.

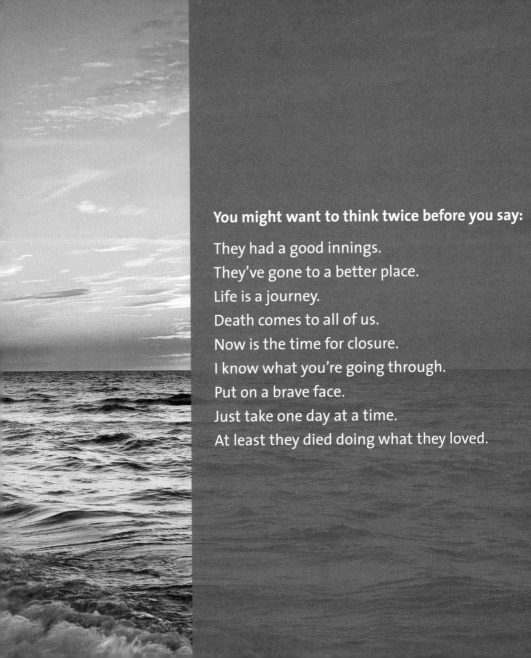

You might want to think twice before you say:

They had a good innings.
They've gone to a better place.
Life is a journey.
Death comes to all of us.
Now is the time for closure.
I know what you're going through.
Put on a brave face.
Just take one day at a time.
At least they died doing what they loved.

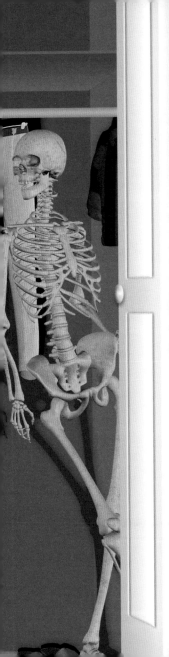

CLEAR THE SKELETONS OUT OF THE CLOSET.

Secret histories often come out when people die,
leaving loved ones confused or wanting
to know more. Consider telling them now.
What have you got to lose?

IN memoriam

DID YOU TELL HER THAT
BEFORE YOU TOLD THE WORLD?

SPROAT. Frances. — On the last day of 1998 Frances Sproat, my Nursie, passed away. Lives weave webs amongst people and one point in that web has physically left us. Through no design of my own, my wonderful Mother selected Nursie to be in my life and was lucky enough to have her look after me as a baby and be loved by her throughout our lives. Her love and care is the most beautiful thing to behold. My love for her is deep and will be with me always. To a wonderful person I give my gratitude for letting me be a small part of you. To her family, especially Betty, I am honoured to know you. — Joanne Lane.

Creek on the 30th
December 1998. Dearly loved
husband of Pamela and loving
father of Brendon and Bronwen

— December 25th 1998. Of Tugun,
Gold Coast. Dearly beloved wife of
Barry. Interred at Tweed Heads
December 30th.
Aged 62 Years

Your dying wish is an opportunity
to make the planet a better place.

going out green

There are a number of eco-friendly ways to honour the lives and beliefs of the deceased. > You can be buried or cremated in a cardboard coffin produced from recycled paper and non-toxic chemicals. > You can be buried at sea, interred vertically to save space, or wrapped in a shroud or biodegradable bodybag. > Green funerals and woodland burials offer the opportunity to plant a tree instead of placing a headstone. > You could go out carbon-neutral by calculating your life's carbon footprint and then leaving money in your will to pay for the equivalent number of trees. > It's a great legacy, clean air.

Good grief. Anger, shock, guilt, sadness, fear, relief, depression. **They're all** might be irritable, distracted or confused, too.

You to be expected and in no particular order. It's all part of the normal grieving process.

If you know someone dealing with the death of a loved one, drop over some

Feed a friend.

groceries or a meal. It's the last thing they'll be thinking about organising.

Going
Underground

The Neanderthals started burying
their dead 70,000 years ago. Egyptians
used sarcophagi, Ancient Greeks used
clay urns, Romans carved coffins out
of limestone and American Indians
buried their dead in canoes or turtle
shells. These days you can be buried
in a coffin, a casket, a basket,
a shroud or a cardboard box.

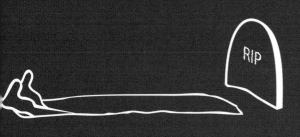

'The best person
to look after someone
who's dying is someone
who loves them.'

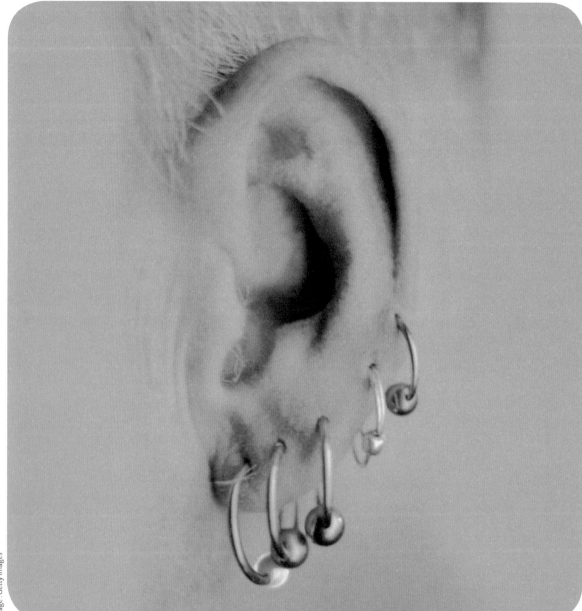

They're handy for listening, too.

Ears are very useful when a friend is grieving. You're not expected to have any answers. *Just listen.*

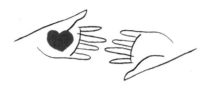

3,538 people in the UK donated organs and tissue in 2008.

At the start of 2009 there were 10,264 people on the transplant waiting list.

That's a long list.

Suicide is a permanent response to what is often a temporary feeling.

Remember their lives, not their deaths.

Memories can fade no matter how hard you try to hold on to them. Record your memories while they're vivid. Write them down, video them or make an audio recording to share with the family.

It's okay

to say their name.*

They're dead;
it doesn't mean
they never existed.

*Except in Indigenous communities, where it can be taboo to mention the deceased by name.

You can be your own funeral director.

Planning and even pre-paying for your own funeral can ease the pressure on your loved ones significantly. And you can farewell everyone in your own style. Find a venue that you like. Pick your favourite music. How about a live band or a DJ? Choose your eulogist. Write the eulogy yourself if you feel like it. Leave the funeral in the sidecar of a Harley. Choose what you want to wear. Eternity is a long time to spend in an ill-fitting suit. It's important for the grieving to have the space to contribute, so try not to overplan. Oh, and tell someone where they can find your instructions.

If you
need me,
I'm here.

If you really mean it, take the initiative.
Often a dying or grieving friend won't
want to ask. All sorts of things can help:
taking their kids to the movies,
cleaning out the fridge, washing the
dishes, mowing their lawn, doing some
ironing, cleaning their bathroom or
putting the washing on the line.
Simple things can be a real relief.

Experts in the great unknown. Many people find faith a source of strength when facing a crisis. It can offer answers or simply a greater awareness of spirituality. You can still talk to priests, reverends, imams, rabbis, elders and other spiritual guides even if you're uncertain about your beliefs. Religious leaders are used to hearing people's doubts and concerns. It's what they do.

Up in smoke

Cremation, the burning of a corpse, can represent either the freeing of the spirit from the body or the prevention of the return of the dead.

Answers to the burning questions.
1. It can take up to 2 hours to cremate a body.
2. The optimum temperature is 900 degrees Celsius.
3. Only one body is cremated at a time – the chamber isn't big enough for more.
4. The fittings are either removed and destroyed or burnt with the coffin.
5. A magnet is used after the cremation to pick out any surgical pins, coffin nails or titanium limbs.
6. Much of the mercury in the atmosphere comes from burning the amalgam fillings in teeth.
7. Bones that do not completely disintegrate can be milled down.
8. In the end the ashes weigh about 2kg.

Cancer 390:1

Heart Disease 410:1

Assault 160,000:1

There's every chance

Falling 10,000:1

Lightning strike 9,000,000: 1

Alzheimer's Disease 8,500:1

HIV 215,000:1

Transport Accident 20,000:1

you're going to die.

*approximations based on UK National Statistics data for 2008

do you have a death

I want to die at home in bed.

wish?

Here are some questions that you may not have asked yourself. **Who would I like to look after me? Where do I want to die, at home or in a hospital? How would I like to be buried? Is there any medical treatment I don't want?** Write down the answers and discuss them with loved ones so they can understand and implement your wishes.

There are many ways to honour the dead.

Build a library. Name a wing. Take a seat. Buy a village a goat, or a well. Plant a tree, or bulbs that come up every year. Name a star. Adopt an animal. Stitch a quilt. Tee off once a year in their honour. Donate to their favourite cause every birthday. Build a monument to love. Set up a perpetual trophy. Fund a scholarship. Buy some bricks. Start a charity. Shake it. Record a song. Observe a moment's silence. Light a candle. Paint them. Learn something from their death.

You have a knack for making me feel really ordinary. Thank you.

Those who are dying often just want to feel normal. It can really help if you do some regular things together. And just be yourselves.

Tell the kids?

Children sense very quickly when something is wrong. If someone close is dying, consider telling the kids – before they start feeling excluded or thinking they are to blame.

Lifting the lid

Historically coffins were made to measure by carpenters or joiners who would undertake to build them, hence the name 'undertakers'. Before refrigeration, flowers were placed around the coffin to mask any unpleasant odours. Funeral 'parlours' were named after the front room in English homes where bodies were traditionally laid out awaiting burial. The term 'wake' is believed to have originated from the practice of creating sufficient racket to determine if someone was really dead or could be woken up. In order to leave the requisite four and a half feet clearance from the coffin lid to the surface, graves had to be about 'six foot deep'.

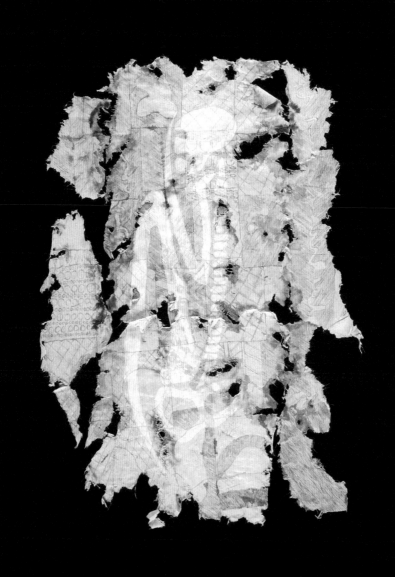

Bones of contention

There are many and varied beliefs around
the world regarding physical and spiritual
responsibilities to those that have passed on. In
Australia one belief that many Aboriginal people
share is that once the deceased is returned to
country through burial rites, they should remain
there. In the past many Aboriginals have been
exhumed and scattered throughout the world as
part of collections. Many Indigenous Australians
have taken on the responsibility of returning their
ancestors to where they belong.

Suddenly they're not there.

Sometimes you don't have the opportunity to say goodbye.

If you're left with things you wanted to say, find a private place, sit down and have a chat.

It's quite normal to speak with the dead.

RIP

YOUR NAME HERE

BORN — DIED

IT'S NOT THE DATES
THAT MATTER,
IT'S THE
DASH
IN BETWEEN.

Jim Henson's funeral was a joyous send-off – everyone was forbidden to wear black and Big Bird sang Kermit's signature song, 'It's not easy being green'. The memorial service was closed with a medley of songs sung by a Muppet choir.

Salvador Dali's final resting place was his last work of art. He was buried beneath the floor of the Teatro-Museo Dali in Figueras, Spain, under an enormous nude of his wife, Gala. Pallbearers and museum guards wore uniforms especially designed by Dali for the occasion. Embalmers claimed that his body would last 300 years.

FUNERALS OF THE

It is believed that 350 million people worldwide watched Winston Churchill's funeral in 1965. Special commentators included Sir Laurence Olivier and former US president Eisenhower. In 1997 an estimated 2 billion people watched the televised funeral of Princess Di.

Despite reports that Mao Zedong preferred cremation, his body was embalmed like the other great communist leaders, Lenin and Stalin, and placed in a glazed mausoleum in Beijing. Every night an elevator lowers his body into a temperature-controlled basement.

When Eva Perón died, a thirty-day mourning period was declared in Argentina. Ministers who did not wear the requisite black armbands and ties were arrested.

RICH AND FAMOUS

Fifty thousand mourners followed the mule-drawn cart that transported the body of Martin Luther King from the funeral to his gravesite. His headstone reads, 'Free at last. Free at last. Thank God Almighty I'm free at last.'

FINANCIAL REVIEW

Only the fittest survive in global automotive jungle

P

The federal government has at least held its nerve on calls to stop the industry to get short-order work

rybody in danger of being 'reckless'

Mum Slept
Peacefully
Last Night

THE ONLY BRISBANE CBD
RIVERFRONT APARTMENTS
RELEASED SINCE 2002

Here are today's headlines.

If you're caring for someone who is dying, it can be handy to prepare an answering machine message for those who call to find out how things are going. Update the machine each day with a ten-second news grab. It will save a lot of exhausting repetition for both of you.

hands on

Therapeutic massage (we're not talking deep tissue or happy endings here) can bring great relief to a dying person. It can also give loved ones something practical to do when they feel really helpless. Of course some patients have medical conditions that may make massage impossible. But for others, touch creates an intimacy that starts people talking.

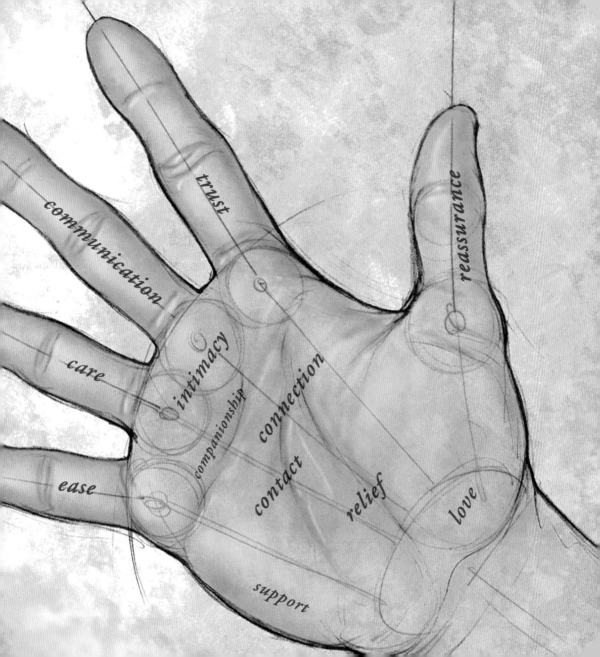

Live on, online.

With your own website you can live on in the virtual world long after you leave the real one. Your friends will have headstones and you'll have a homepage.

Setting up a website is an ideal way of being remembered for the things that are important to you. Include your favourite snaps. Write your own history or tell it with podcasts. You could even leave messages for the next generation. Think of your website as a time capsule or a portal to eternal life.

N A
I I
T N

Don't just sit there.

☑ Read me the newspaper or a book.
☐ Do the crossword with me.
☑ Check the football score.
☑ Hold my hand.
☐ Help me write a letter.
☑ Light the incense.
☑ Find some music I like.
☐ Tell me a joke. Please.
☐ Tell me another one.

☑ *Don't overstay your welcome.*

TODAY'S TARGET 14
21 words, very goo
excellent. See solut

YESTERDAY'S SOLUTI
carte cater cite cra
gait gaiter garret ga
GERIATRIC girt grat
irate irrigate rate re
tier tiger tire trace
trier trig

ters
n those
ay be
word
tter
one
ending
o proper
ST

RATED:

3 Saying, 'Shun ch
has a premonitio
4 One country to b
air, below 51 (7
5 Travel guide yet
cryptic (6,9)
6 Low sound rises
plea for alcohol
7 Lawgiver, holdin
organises the w
8 Cruelly sneered
certain requiren
9 So, Lily circled
'Quo?' in a con
herself (9)
13 Starts talking a
weaving in a w
15 Talk on water i
estate (7)
19 In initially han
that's barbaric
20 Doing badly u
colour (6)
23 I had assume
did nothing (5

SOLUTIO

Maybe I don't want to get over it.

Some say you never stop grieving for a loved one. You just get used to the idea of not having them around. So saying, 'Time heals all wounds' or 'You'll get over it' might be exactly the wrong thing to say.

A funeral can be a celebration of a life well lived.

Location. It can be somewhere unexpected: the beach, a football pitch, your garden.

Music. Play something jubilant. You could make a compilation of the deceased's favourite songs for everyone.

Readings. They don't have to be psalms. You can read letters from the deceased, or recite poems or excerpts from books they loved.

Eulogy. Don't be afraid to make people laugh.

Reminders. You can commemorate the dead by handing out personal keepsakes at the funeral: a stem of their favourite flower, a bulb to take home and plant, a golf ball with their initials on it. You might ask friends and family to record their memories of the deceased in a journal.

Personal touches. It's important to remain faithful to the memory of the deceased. Have balloons instead of flowers if that's what they would have preferred. Dress them in their Batman suit if that's what they asked for. There are no rules.

There's no right or wrong way to grieve.

People mourn in different ways. Sometimes it's according to religious or spiritual codes. Often it is more personalised. It just depends. Let them grieve in a way that feels right for them, free of expectation and pressure. **It might be harder than it sounds.**

IF THEY'RE DYING,

THEY'RE ABOUT TO LOSE EVERYTHING: RELATIONSHIPS, HOME, DIGNITY, HEALTH, FAVOURITE BOOKS, SUNDAY SLEEP-INS, BEACH HOLIDAYS, WINE, LONG WALKS, FRIENDS, GOING OUT TO DINNER, BUILDING BONFIRES, KISSES, OVERSEAS TRIPS, BARBEQUED SAUSAGES, ASSETS, READING BEDTIME STORIES, BIRTHDAYS, ALL-TIME FAVOURITE ALBUM

CHILDREN LAUGHING, THE SMELL OF MOWN GRASS, BREATHING SEA AIR, DODGING RAIN SHOWERS, SUNRISES AND SUNSETS, WIND IN THEIR HAIR,

EVERYTHING.

Expect them to be a bit grumpy from time to time.

I feel
like
talking
about it.

Mary was born just after World War I in the tiny village of Bruton in Somerset. 🌺 She was the school high-jump champion and competed in the county finals. 🌺 She used to ride to school on her horse with both her brothers on board. They laughed all the way there most mornings until Arthur fell off and broke his arm. 🌺 Mary trained as a nurse and in World War II was parachuted into France to help the French Resistance. She saved the lives of dozens of escaping prisoners. 🌺 She met the prime minister Sir Winston Churchill once. And Lady Di. She preferred Lady Di. 🌺 Her favourite dance is the samba, which she is still pretty good at. 🌺

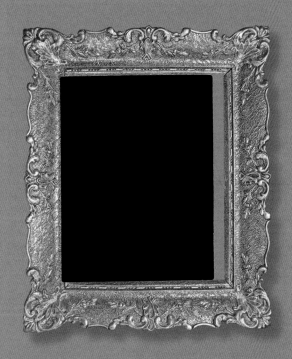

Mary has done lots of things
that no one ever asks
her about. 🌼

Image · Getty Images

Dad,

what does 'dead' mean?

Questions like this often come up when kids
are trying to understand the death of a pet,
a member of the extended family or someone from
school. Generally children need simple, gentle and
honest answers, and lots of reassurance.

Invitation

Please come to my wake.
No, I'm not dead yet.
I just want to see all my friends
and loved ones before I am.
Come and enjoy my favourite food,
a celebratory drink and
some bangin' beats.

Throw your own wake.

It's not
crazy to set
an extra place
at the table.

If you're missing someone, especially at a family get-together like a birthday or anniversary, set a place for them. Pour their favourite drink and tell stories about them. You'll probably all cry but that's normal.

Death just might be the start of something wonderful.

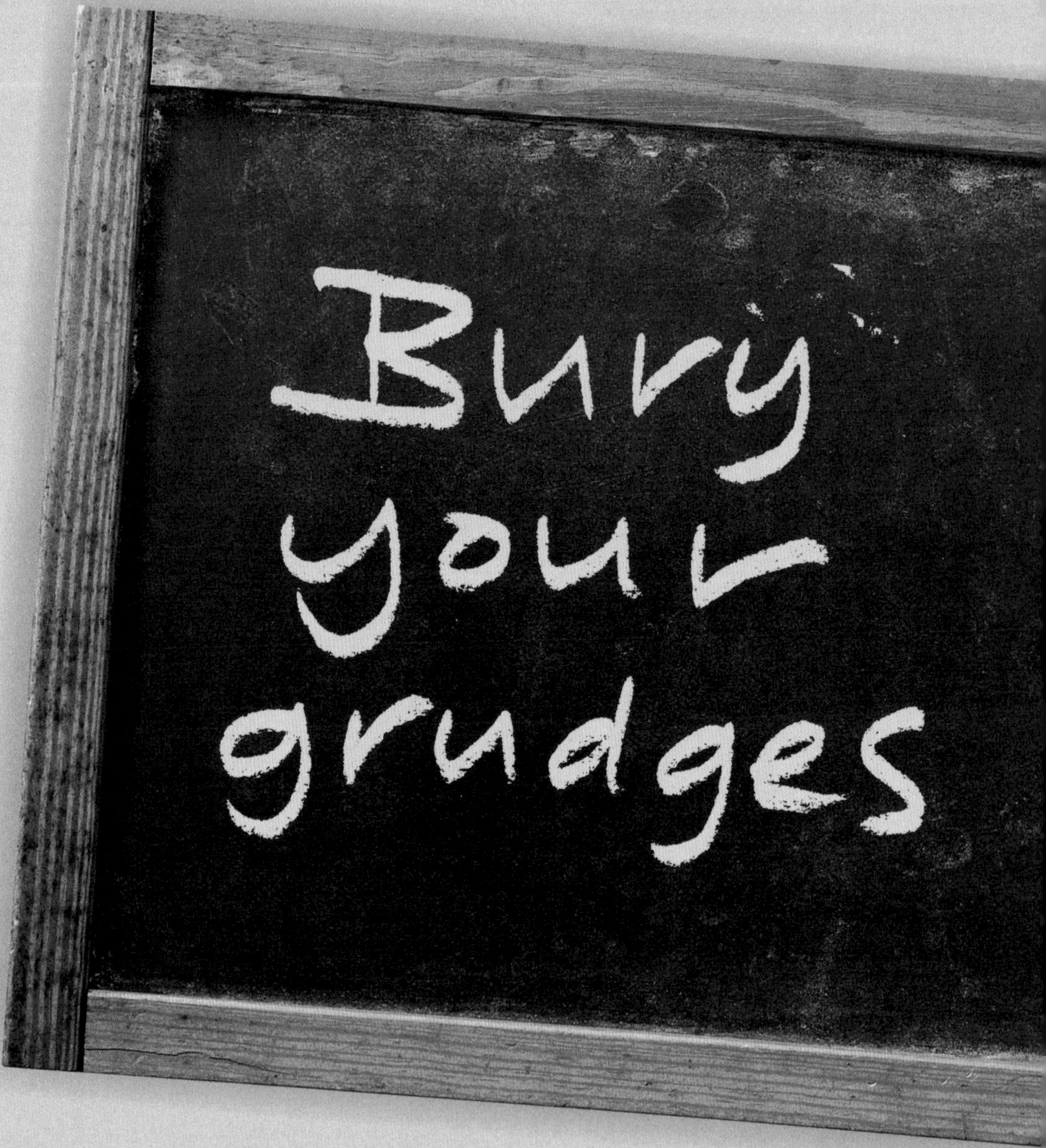

Image: iStockphoto

I want to go out with a clean slate.
No grudges and no hard feelings.

unnatural
causes

456 B.C.
- Legend has it that Aeschylus, the ancient Greek playwright, died when an eagle mistook his head for a rock and dropped a tortoise on him.

260
- When the Persian king Shapur I captured the Roman emperor Valerian, he used him as a footstool and then had him skinned and stuffed with straw.

1477
- It was rumoured that when presented with a choice in execution techniques, George Plantagenet elected to be drowned and the sentence was carried out in a barrel of wine.

1911 • french tailor franz reichelt died testing his revolutionary 'coat parachute' off the eiffel tower.

1911 • whiskey baron jack daniel died from blood poisoning. tennessee folklore has it that he bruised his toe kicking a safe whose combination he had forgotten.

1980 • ac/dc lead singer bon scott choked on his own vomit.

1983 • american playwright tennessee williams choked on a bottle cap.

2007 • it was reported that american jennifer strange died of water intoxication trying to win a nintendo wii in a 'hold your wii' competition.

TYING UP LOOSE ENDS
DOESN'T MEAN
YOU'RE GIVING UP.

✓ Write a will.
✓ Consider a power of attorney.
✓ Arrange to close bank accounts.
✓ Cancel credit cards.
✓ Notify pension companies.
✓ Tell health insurers.
✓ Make a list of outstanding debtors and creditors.
✓ Find a carer for your pets.
✓ Redirect the mail.
✓ Put all these important documents together in a box and tell someone where it is.

Keep i̇

People often feel
lonely after someone
they love dies.

touch.

You can help them feel less isolated just by staying in touch, in any way that feels right. There's the phone, email, SMS, Skype, webcam, visiting, telex, telegraph, sign language, carrier pigeon, postcard, fax or a note under their door. Even if it's just to say, 'Hi, I'm thinking about you.'

Leave an emotional will.

Among all the things you leave
your loved ones – shares, the couch,
the Turkish rug – why not leave them
something from the heart?
Leave your family your love,
or bequeath your friends a joke.

*Grief
is the price
we pay for
intimacy.*

Death is the destination we all share. *anon* Remembering that I'll be dead soon is the most important tool I've ever encountered to help me make the big choices in life. *Steve Jobs* A man's dying is more the survivors' affair than his own. *Thomas Mann*, The Magic Mountain Death may be the greatest of all human blessings. *Socrates* Death never takes the wise man by surprise; He is always ready to go. *Jean de La Fontaine* Death is caused by swallowing small amounts of saliva over a long period of time. *Attributed to George Carlin* People living deeply have no fear of death. *Anaïs Nin, Diary, 1967* Death is beautiful when seen to be a law, and not an accident. It is as common as life. *Henry David Thoreau, 11 March 1842, letter to Ralph Waldo Emerson* I wanted a perfect ending. Now I've learned, the hard way, that some poems don't rhyme, and some stories don't have a clear beginning, middle, and end. Life is about not knowing, having to change, taking the moment and making the best of it, without knowing what's going to happen next. Delicious ambiguity. *Gilda Radner* I am ready to meet my Maker. Whether my Maker is prepared for the great ordeal of meeting me is another matter. *Winston Churchill* I've got a great ambition to die of exhaustion rather than boredom. *Angus Grossart* Our lives begin to end the day we become silent about things that matter. *Martin Luther King* We are here to laugh at the odds and live our lives so well that Death will tremble to take us. *Charles Bukowski* Health nuts are going to feel stupid someday, lying in hospitals dying of nothing. *Redd Foxx* They say such nice things about people at their funerals that it makes me sad that I'm going to miss mine by just a few days. *Garrison Kielor.* If you should die before me ... can you ask to bring a friend? *Unknown* The really frightening thing about middle age is the knowledge that you'll grow out of it. *Doris Day* I intend to live forever. So far, so good. *Steven Wright* The idea is to die young as late as possible. *Ashley Montagu* Love — is anterior to Life — Posterior — to Death — Initial of Creation, and The Exponent of Earth. *Emily Dickinson* Live as if you were to die tomorrow. Learn as if you were to live forever. *Mahatma Gandhi* The fear of death follows from the fear of life. A man who lives fully is prepared to die at any time. *Mark Twain* Men fear Death, as children fear to go in the dark; and as that natural fear in children is increased with tales, so is the other. *Francis Bacon*, Essays Oh, for the time when I shall sleep without identity. *Emily Brontë* The graveyards are full of indispensable men. *Charles de Gaulle* The goal of all life is death. *Sigmund Freud* To the psychotherapist an old man who cannot bid farewell to life appears as feeble and sickly as a young man who is unable to embrace it. *C.G. Jung* No one knows whether death is really the greatest blessing a man can have, but they fear it is the greatest curse, as if they knew well. *Plato* After all, to the well-organized mind, death is but the next great adventure. *J.K. Rowling* Life and death are balanced on the edge of a razor. *Homer*, Iliad Death is for many of us the gate of hell; but we are inside on the way out, not outside on the way in. *George Bernard Shaw* From my rotting body, flowers shall grow and I am in them and that is eternity. *Edvard Munch* People do not die for us immediately, but remain bathed in a sort of aura of life which bears no relation to true immortality but through which they continue to occupy our thoughts in the same way as when they were alive. It is as though they were traveling abroad. *Marcel Proust* 'Tis very certain the desire of life prolongs it. *Lord Byron* Who chants a doleful hymn to his own death? *Shakespeare* Death leaves a heartache no one can heal, love leaves a memory no one can steal. *Unknown*

No one can confidently say that he will still be living tomorrow. *Euripides* While I thought that I was learning how to live, I have been learning how to die. *Leonardo Da Vinci* God himself took a day to rest in, and a good man's grave is his Sabbath. *John Donne* Our death is not an end if we can live on in our children and the younger generation. For they are us, our bodies are only wilted leaves on the tree of life. *Albert Einstein* Death may be the greatest of all human blessings. *Socrates* Time rushes towards us with its hospital tray of infinitely varied narcotics, even while it is preparing us for its inevitably fatal operation. *Tennessee Williams*, The Rose Tattoo He who has gone, so we but cherish his memory, abides with us, more potent, nay, more present than the living man. *Antoine de Saint Éxupéry* Hope is grief's best music. *anon* The courage of life is often a less dramatic spectacle than the courage of the final moment; but it is no less a magnificent mixture of triumph and tragedy. *John F. Kennedy* Patience makes lighter what sorrow may not heal. *Horace* In the midst of winter, I found there was, within me, an invincible summer. *Albert Camus* My sun sets to rise again. *Robert Browning* He not busy being born is busy dying. *Bob Dylan* I hope the leaving is joyful; and I hope never to return. *Frida Kahlo* For three days after death hair and fingernails continue to grow but phone calls taper off. *Johnny Carson* There are worse things in life than death. Have you ever spent an evening with an insurance salesman? *Woody Allen* Life isn't fair. It's just fairer than death, that's all. *William Goldman*, The Princess Bride To be idle is a short road to death and to be diligent is a way of life; foolish people are idle, wise people are diligent. *Buddha* When you're dead, you're dead. That's it. *Marlene Dietrich* Alas, I am dying beyond my means. *Oscar Wilde* The trouble with quotes about death is that 99.999 percent of them are made by people who are still alive. *Joshua Bruns* Thank Heaven! the crisis — The danger, is past, and the lingering illness, is over at last, and the fever called "Living" is conquered at last. *Edgar Allan Poe* I know one day I'll turn the corner and I won't be ready for it. *Jean-Michel Basquiat* 100 per cent of us die, and the percentage cannot be increased. *C.S. Lewis*, The Weight of Glory To fear death, gentlemen, is no other than to think oneself wise when one is not, to think one knows what one does not know. No one knows whether death may not be the greatest of all blessings for a man, yet men fear it as if they knew that it is the greatest of evils. And surely it is the most blameworthy ignorance to believe that one knows what one does not know. *Plato* From the hour you're born you begin to die. But between birth and death there's life. *Simone de Beauvoir*, All Men Art Mortal When we are at the end of life, to die means to go away; when we are at the beginning, to go away means to die. *Victor Hugo*, Les Misérables In an artist's life, death is perhaps not the most difficult thing. *Vincent van Gogh* How do our lives ravel out into the no-wind, no-sound, the weary gestures wearily recapitulant: echoes of old compulsions with no-hand on no-strings: in sunset we fall into furious attitudes, dead gestures of dolls. *William Faulkner*, As I Lay Dying I live now on borrowed time, waiting in the anteroom for the summons that will inevitably come. And then — I go on to the next thing, whatever it is. One doesn't luckily have to bother about that. *Agatha Christie* Even in the desolate wilderness, stars can still shine. *Aoi Jiyuu Shiroi Nozomi* Death must be so beautiful. To lie in the soft brown earth, with the grasses waving above one's head, and listen to silence. To have no yesterday, and no tomorrow. To forget time, to forgive life, to be at peace. *Oscar Wilde*

YOUR SPARE

1. Transplants save lives. In 2008, 977 lives in the UK were saved through a heart, lung, liver or combined transplant.

2. You can donate your heart, liver, lungs, kidneys and pancreas, as well as tissue such as your corneas, bone, heart valves and skin.

3. Your organs won't be harvested until you are declared dead. In fact, if you are donating your organs, more tests than usual are carried out to determine that you are truly dead.

4. If you are a registered organ donor, emergency staff work just as hard to save your life. Your doctor won't switch your life-support off prematurely. Their priority is to keep you alive.

5. Medical students don't use you for practice. Organ donating is not the same as leaving your body to science. No donated tissue or organs are used for research without your explicit permission.

PARTS COULD

6. It's not a Tarantino film. Donated organs and tissue are recovered by professional medical staff, like any normal operation. Donors' bodies are always treated with respect and dignity.

7. You'll still look like you at the funeral. Donating organs doesn't alter your physical appearance.

8. Don't assume that you are too old or unfit to be a donor. To a 60-year-old, a 50-year-old heart is a bonus.

9. You should tell your family. It is important to discuss your plans to donate your organs with your immediate family so they know your intentions.

10. The NHS Organ Donor Register is a simple way of recording your decision to become a donor.

SAVE A LIFE

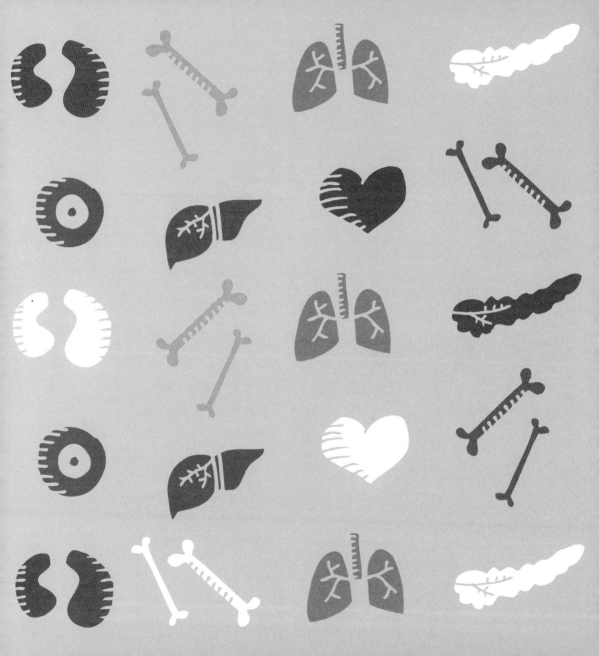

The other kind of stiff

Life-threatening illnesses, and their treatments, can often affect your self-image. You may feel physically unattractive because of surgery, hair loss, tiredness or nausea. You might be afraid of being rejected by your partner, so you're avoiding sexual contact. Maybe they don't want to place demands on you? If you have fears or doubts about your love-making, try discussing them with your partner. Who knows where the social intercourse might lead?

They're deceased.
That doesn't make them a saint.

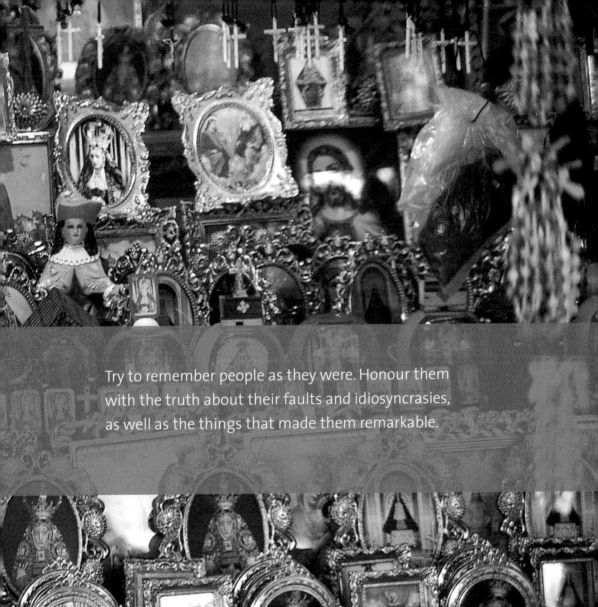

Try to remember people as they were. Honour them with the truth about their faults and idiosyncrasies, as well as the things that made them remarkable.

Why do some cultures
have elders but others
have the elderly?

Grief has no measure.

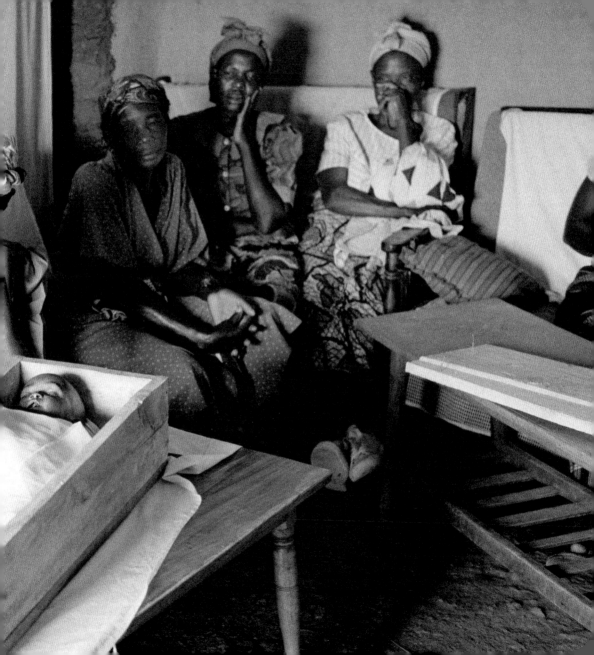

WHAT'S YOUR HURRY?

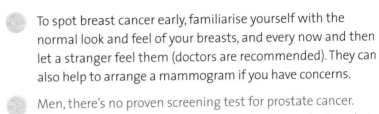 To spot breast cancer early, familiarise yourself with the normal look and feel of your breasts, and every now and then let a stranger feel them (doctors are recommended). They can also help to arrange a mammogram if you have concerns.

Men, there's no proven screening test for prostate cancer. So you need to pull your finger out and ask your doctor what to look out for.

Drive like a loved one is coming the other way. Someone's is.

Don't forget, about 75% of the world's surface is covered in water. Teach your kids to swim.

Learn mouth-to-mouth and CPR. We can all be lifesavers.

There's no screening test for ovarian cancer yet, but if you are over 50 or have a family history of ovarian cancer you may be at greater risk. Ask your doctor about symptoms to watch for.

With diabetes 2 you can eat your way into an early grave.

That beauty spot won't seem so beautiful if it turns out to be a melanoma. So be SunSmart and watch for changes in spots on your skin.

If you smoke cigarettes you're playing with fire. About 250 people in the UK die from smoking every day. It may not be easy, but there's a simple way to avoid being one of them.

www.sja.org.uk
www.mariecurie.org.uk
www.diabetes.org.uk

You're not dead yet!

Weblinks you might find interesting, after reading this book:

Age Concern	www.ageconcern.org.uk
Alzheimer's Society	www.alzheimers.org.uk
Bereavement UK	www.bereavement.co.uk
Breast Cancer Care	www.breastcancercare.org.uk
Cancer Chat	www.cancerchat.org.uk
Cancer Research UK	www.cancerresearchuk.org.uk
Carers UK	www.carersuk.org
Caring for children with cancer	www.clicsargent.org.uk
Childhood Bereavement Network	www.childhoodbereavementnetwork.org.uk
Citizens Advice Bureau	www.citizensadvice.org.uk
Community Legal Advice	www.communitylegaladvice.org.uk
Crossroads Care	www.crossroads.org.uk
Cruse Bereavement Care	www.crusebereavementcare.org.uk
Death Online	www.deathonline.net
Department of Health	www.dh.gov.uk
Debt Advice Trust	www.debtadvicetrust.org.uk
Diabetes UK	www.diabetes.org.uk
Dying Matters Coalition	www.dyingmatters.org
Dying to Know	www.pilotlight.org.au
Help the Aged	www.helptheaged.org.uk
Help the Hospices	www.helpthehospices.org.uk
Macmillan Cancer Support	www.macmillan.org.uk
Marie Curie Cancer Care	www.mariecurie.org.uk
National Association of Funeral Directors	www.nafd.org.uk
National Association of Widows	www.nawidows.org.uk
National Council for Palliative Care	www.ncpc.org.uk

National End of Life Care Programme	www.endoflifecareforadults.nhs.uk/eolc/
Natural Death Centre	www.naturaldeath.org.uk
NHS Direct	www.nhsdirect.nhs.uk/
Online coaching and mentoring network	www.horsesmouth.co.uk
Ovarian Cancer Action	www.ovarian.org.uk
Papyrus – prevention of young suicide	www.papyrus-uk.org
The Princess Royal Trust for Carers	www.carers.org
The Prostate Cancer Charity	www.prostate-cancer.org.uk
Quakers Social Action	www.quakersocialaction.com
Samaritans	www.samaritans.org
St John Ambulance	www.sja.org.uk
Sue Ryder Care	www.suerydercare.org
TimeBank	www.timebank.org.uk
Turn 2 Us	www.turn2us.org.uk
UK Transplant	www.uktransplant.org.uk
Volunteering England	www.volunteering.org.uk
Will People	www.willpeople.co.uk
Young Carers	www.youngcarers.net

Many people and organisations have contributed to the creation of this book.
Pilotlight Australia would especially like to thank:

Freehills and our legal eagle **Alice Macdougall**

Hardie Grant Books in Australia and the UK for their help in sales, marketing and editorial

Simon Longstaff and **Tim Costello** for their wisdom and guidance

Hoyne Design for their work on concepts and development.

The Knight, Anastasios, Lane and Exton families

The Australian Government for support in printing the first edition of the book.

Alex McDonald
Alice Welbourn
Andrew Hoyne
Banu Erzurun
Ben Padfield
Brian Sweeney
Carolan Davidge
Caroline Guerin
Charles Lane
Community Links UK
Darren Heveren
David Robinson
Della Hannon
Dianne Anastasios
Edward Mackay
Emma Schwarcz
Geoff Mulgan
Helen Ferguson
Hugo Tewson
Ian Smith
Jackie Polonsky
James Anastasios
Jane Anastasios

Jane Aspden
Jane Beaton
Jane Halton
Jean Oelwang
Jennifer Lalor
Jim O'Neill
Jim Stynes
Joanne Wood
Joel Joffe
Judith Moran
Julia Cleverdon
Julian Lincoln
Julie Pinkham
Katherine Kordanovski
Kyah Woodhill
Kerry Hancock
Koorie Heritage Trust
Leo Campbell
Linda Morrison
Matthew Anastasios
Meaghan Wilson-Anastasios
Melissa Razuki
Michael Hirsh

Michelle Mackintosh
Noel Lane
Pacific Brands
Palliative Care Australia
Paul Woodward
Peter Houghton
Peter Scott
River Capital
Rob Sitch
Ron Dewhurst
Sandy Grant
Shannon Faulkhead
Stephen Jacobs
Steve Hancock
Sue Anastasios
Sue Hale
Suzi Carp
Therese van Maanen
The Age
Trisha Garner
Vanessa Howe